Endangered Species

By Marilynn Martin

a coloring book devoted to endangered animals

ISBN 978-0-578-46078-9

List of animals in the order in which they appear in the book

Horned Puffin

Amur Leopard

Saola

Beluga Whale

Malayan Tiger

Red Wolf

Sea Otter

Bactrian Camel

African Penguin

Indian Pangolin

Scottish Wildcat

Asian Elephant

African Rhino

Monarch Butterfly

Hawksbill Sea Turtle

Green Iguana

White-Cheeked Gibbon

European Mink

Andean Flamingo

Slow Loris

Koala

Tips

Use the test pages for testing colors,
different media and blending

To prevent bleeding or transfer,
place a thick piece of paper under
the coloring page you are working on

If you have enjoyed this book
or it has touched you in some way
use #endangeredspeciesmartin

Merchandise is also available in my shop
Nins Art Cabinet on Zazzle

Test Page

Test Page

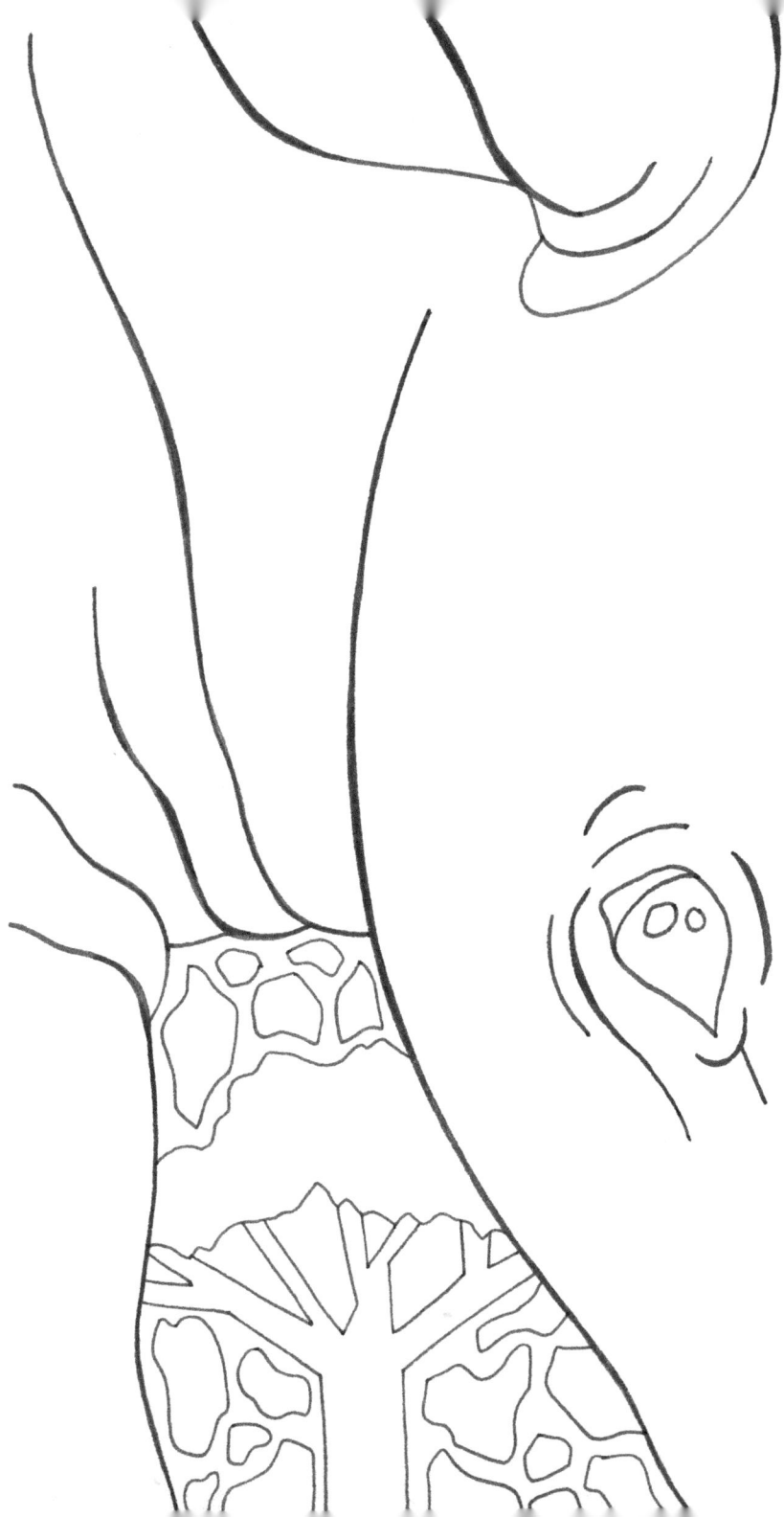

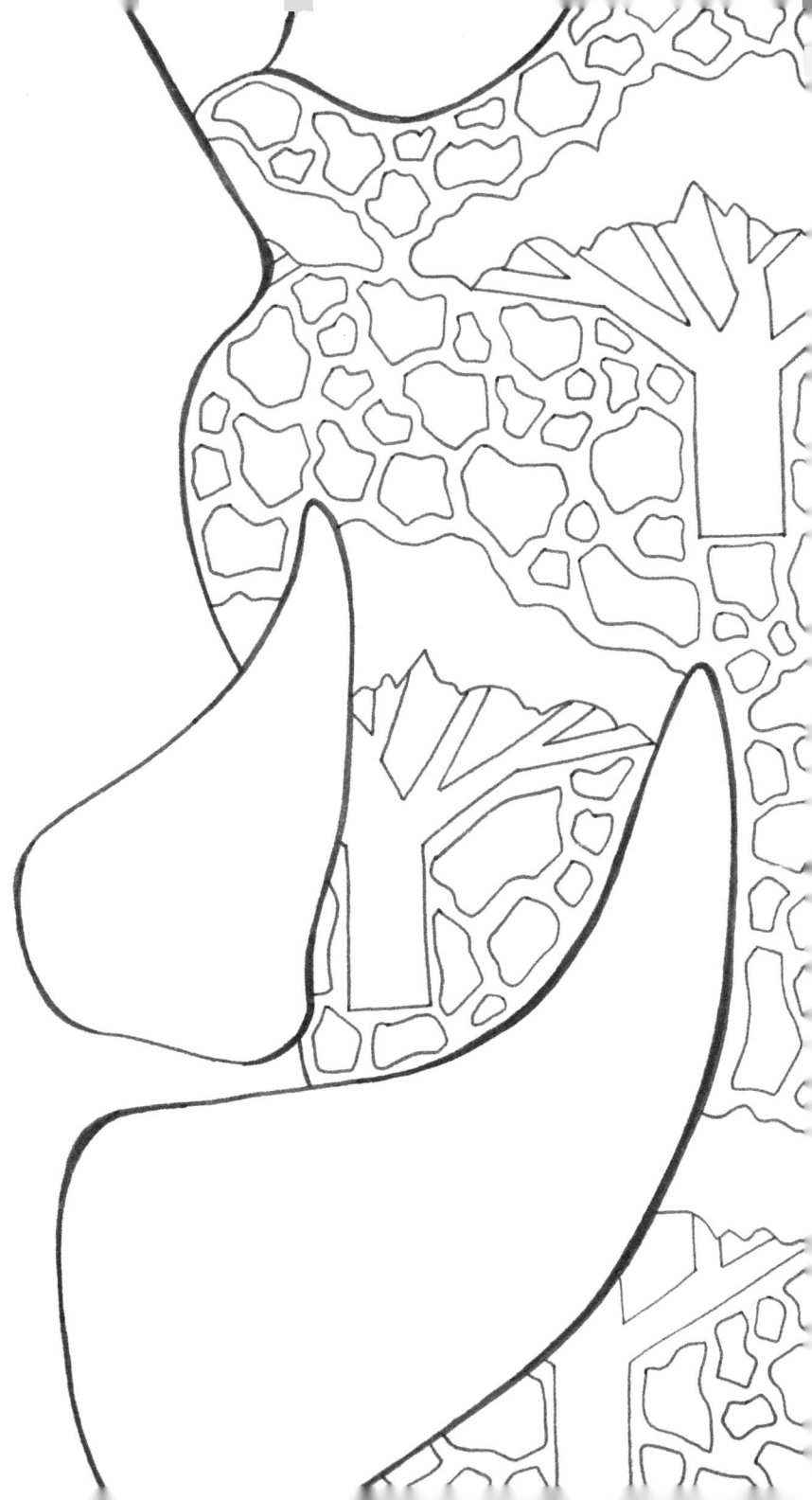

Test Page

Congratulations!

This certificate is to commend

_____

Name   **Date**

**for completing Endangered Species
a coloring book devoted to endangered animals**